How Artists Use
COLOUR

Paul Flux

Heinemann
LIBRARY

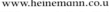
www.heinemann.co.uk
Visit our website to find out more information about **Heinemann Library** books.

To order:
 Phone 44 (0) 1865 888066
 Send a fax to 44 (0) 1865 314091
 Visit the Heinemann Bookshop at www.heinemann.co.uk to browse our catalogue and order online.

First published in Great Britain by Heinemann Library, Halley Court, Jordan Hill, Oxford OX2 8EJ,
a division of Reed Educational and Professional Publishing Ltd.
Heinemann is a registered trademark of Reed Educational and Professional Publishing Ltd.

OXFORD MELBOURNE AUCKLAND JOHANNESBURG BLANTYRE
GABORONE IBADAN PORTSMOUTH (NH) USA CHICAGO

© Reed Educational and Professional Publishing Ltd 2002

Designed by Celia Floyd
Illustrations by Jo Brooker/Ann Miller
Originated by Ambassador Litho Ltd
Printed and bound by South China Printing in Hong Kong/China

ISBN 0 431 16200 X (hardback)   ISBN 0 431 16205 0 (paperback)
06 05 04 03 02   06 05 04 03 02
10 9 8 7 6 5 4 3 2 1   10 9 8 7 6 5 4 3 2 1

British Library Cataloguing in Publication Data

Flux, Paul
    How artists use colour. (Take-off!)
    1. Colour in art – Juvenile literature
    I. Title
    701.8'5

Acknowledgements

The publishers would like to thank the following for permission to reproduce photographs:

AKG, London: pp7, 9, 14, 17, AKG, London / DACS pp19,27; Bridgeman Art Library: pp12, 18, National Gallery of Scotland, Edinburgh / DACS p16, Peter Willi p11; Trevor Clifford / Jo Booker: pp23, 24, 25; Corbis: National Gallery, London p28; DACS 2000 The Museum of Modern Art, New York: p20; Bookmalli Aboriginal Artists. Purchased with the assistance of funds from National Gallery admission charges and commisioned in 1987. Collection; National Gallery of Australia, Canberra: p15; SCALA: p10; Tate Gallery, London / DACS: p13.

Cover photograph reproduced with permission of Bridgeman Art Library/Richard Miller Collection.

Our thanks to Sue Graves and Hilda Reed for their advice and expertise in the preparation of this book.

Every effort has been made to contact copyright holders of any material reproduced in this book. Any omissions will be rectified in subsequent printings if
notice is given to the publishers.

Contents

Any words appearing in the text in bold, **like this**, are explained in the Glossary.

Making colours

Our eyes can see thousands of colours, some bright, some of them dark. Red, yellow and blue are called **primary colours**. They cannot be made by mixing together other colours.

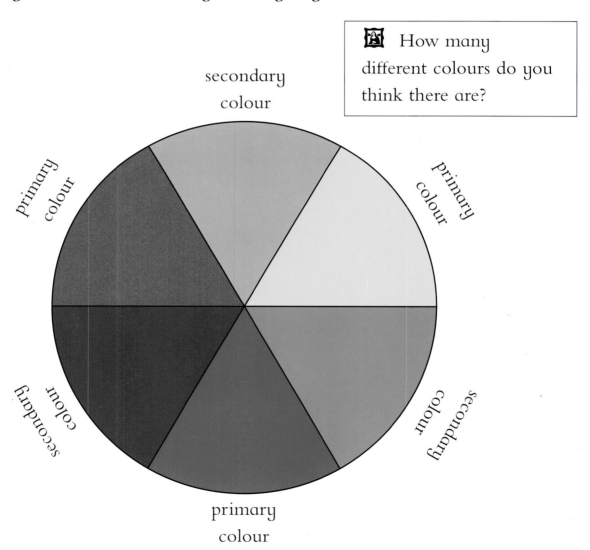

How many different colours do you think there are?

secondary colour

primary colour

primary colour

secondary colour

secondary colour

primary colour

Primary colours can be mixed to make every other colour.

Secondary colours are made by mixing two primary colours together. By adding more of one colour you get different **shades**. If you mix all three primary colours together you get a muddy brown!

You mix two primary colours together to make secondary colours.

blue + yellow = green

blue + red = purple

red + yellow = orange

Did you know that many animals do not see any colours?

red + blue + yellow = brown

Colour partners

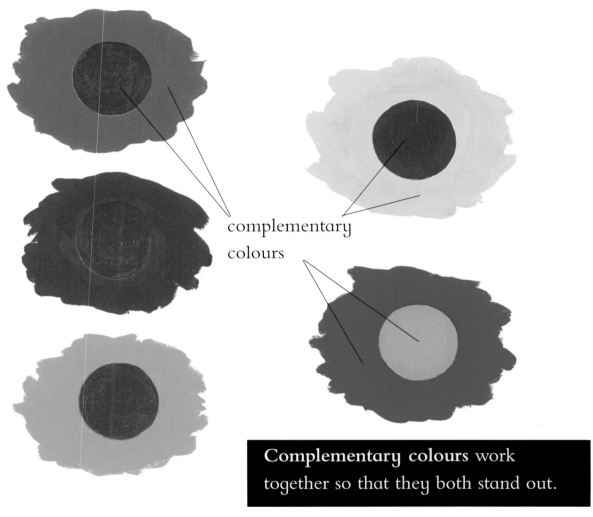

complementary colours

Complementary colours work together so that they both stand out.

Look at the colour wheel on page 4 again. Opposite colours **complement** one another. This means that they both stand out. Look at the red blobs on this page. All three are exactly the same but the one on the green background seems much brighter than the others.

Vincent van Gogh was a Dutch painter who lived from 1853 to 1890.

green background

dark hat

wavy beard

dark coat

Vincent van Gogh, *Portrait of the Postman Joseph Roulin*, 1889.

Van Gogh is well known for his use of complementary colours. The face of the postman stands out because the green background **contrasts** with the dark hat and coat and the wavy beard.

Warm and cool colours

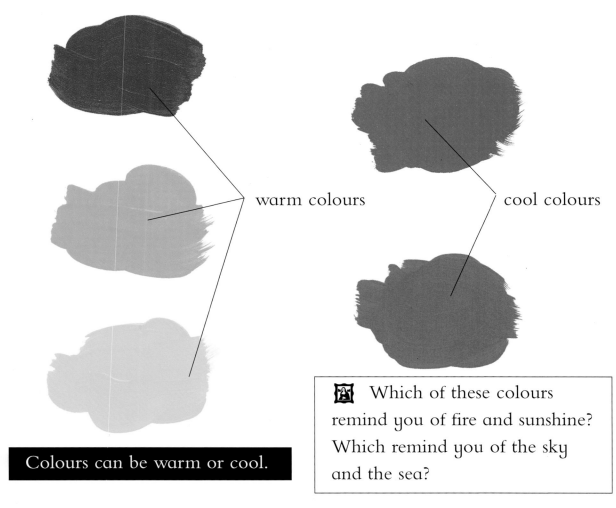

warm colours

cool colours

Colours can be warm or cool.

Which of these colours remind you of fire and sunshine? Which remind you of the sky and the sea?

Warm colours are red, yellow and orange. Often artists use these colours to show strong feelings. Cool colours are blue and green. When artists use cool colours their pictures can seem cold and lacking in feeling.

8

The French artist Paul Cézanne used warm colours to give his pictures great strength. Here he has put fruit on a white cloth with **earth colours** around it. The warm colours make the ordinary objects seem extra special.

Warm colours bring a **scene** to life.

cloth   apples   jug

Paul Cézanne, *Apples and Oranges*, 1895-1900.

Colour makes a difference!

hieroglyphs

This picture shows Egyptian hieroglyphic letters.

Can you make your writing more interesting by using different colours?

Look at these ancient Egyptian letters, which we call **hieroglyphs**. The walls of the tombs of kings were often covered with writing like this. The yellows, greens and browns make the writing more **decorative**.

Rose Window, Notre Dame Cathedral, Paris, France, about 1250.

Look at the date of this window. How old is it?

Stained glass has been used in churches for hundreds of years. Light is flooding through the glass in this window and filling the inside of the church with bright colours. People standing beneath the window can be covered with rainbow colours.

How artists use colour

Artists use colour in many ways. This painting is by an artist called Mark Rothko. He used big blocks of colour with fuzzy edges to show different moods and feelings. This kind of art is called **abstract**. It uses only colour and shape to make the picture.

Mark Rothko, *White Cloud Over Purple*, 1957.

How does this painting make you feel?

Henri Matisse made this picture when he was over 80 years old. His helpers painted large sheets of paper, and Matisse cut them into shapes and then stuck them onto **canvas**. He wanted to **explore** the difference between drawing objects, and making them with colour.

> 🖼 Why do you think Matisse called this picture *The Snail*?

Henri Matisse, *The Snail*, 1953.

Colour adds meaning

angel Gabriel

Mary

Fra Angelico, *The Annunciation,* 1437–45.

In this painting, the angel Gabriel is telling Mary that she will give birth to Jesus, the Son of God. Look closely at Gabriel's wings. The blue and orange feathers **complement** one another, and so do the red clothes and green grass. Here colour is being used to help express deep religious feelings.

In Australia, around 200 years ago, the **Aboriginals** had their land taken from them by people from Europe. In the 1980s a group of 43 artists made this forest of hollow log bone-coffins. It shows ancient **designs** in natural **earth colours** to celebrate the Aboriginal culture.

Some of these hollow log bone-coffins are more than 3 metres tall. Measure 3 metres to see how big they are.

Ramingining Artists, *The Aboriginal Memorial*, 1987-88.

Colours in balance

The French artist Claude Monet was interested in the effect of light. He painted many pictures of the same places at different times of the day. In this beautiful painting he has balanced the blue light of early evening in winter, with an orange sky. This creates a feeling of great peace.

Claude Monet, *Haystacks: Snow Effect,* 1891.

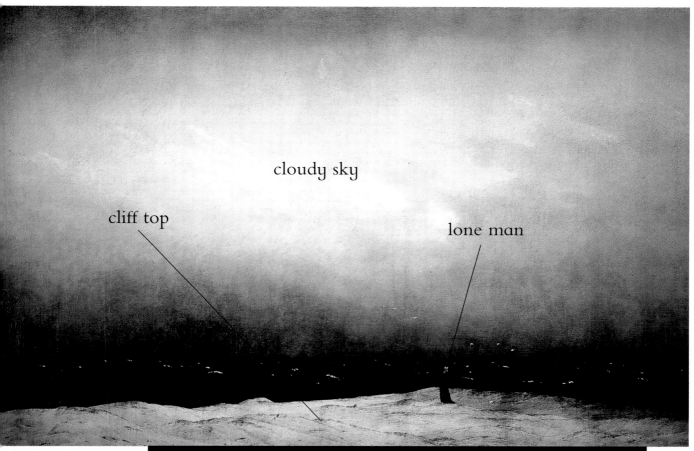

cloudy sky

cliff top

lone man

Caspar David Friedrich, *The Monk by the Sea*, 1808-10.

In this painting we can see a cloudy sky reflected on the a bare cliff top. The blue **tones** weave together to give a feeling of space. The lone man seems so small, set against the huge sky.

Colours that shout!

Joan Miró, *Figures in the Night*, 1960.

Think about the title of this painting. Would you want to be alone on a night like this?

Colours can be used in ways which surprise us. In this picture, dark night-time shapes are surrounded by strong splashes of colour which seem to leap off the **canvas**. But these bright **tones** are held in check by a mysterious darkness.

18

Edvard Munch, *The Scream*, 1893.

Bold colours are used again here, to make the painting strong.
Swirling **shades** of red and orange push out from the **canvas**.
The bright colours add to the excitement of the painting.

Colour and the modern world

This was one of Piet Mondrian's last paintings. All his life he **experimented** with the **primary colours**. He painted **abstract** pictures using yellow, red and blue. He also used grey and white blocks, and black lines to separate them.

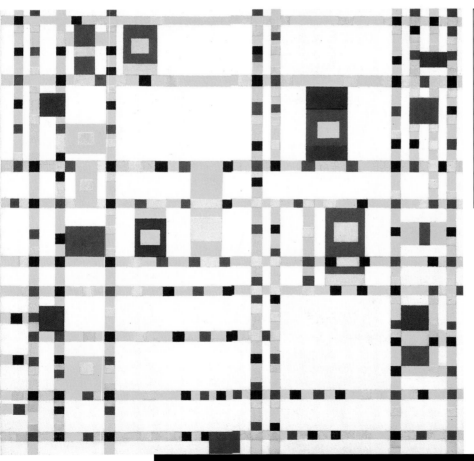

The straight lines of New York City's streets gave Mondrian the idea for this painting.

Piet Mondrian, *Broadway Boogie Woogie*, 1942-43.

Did you know that you can use the computer to send pictures you have made to a friend in another country? Have you ever done this?

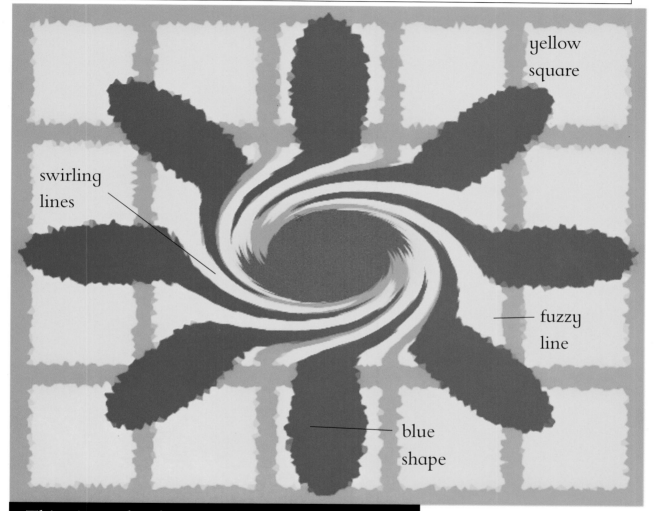

yellow square

swirling lines

fuzzy line

blue shape

This picture has been made using a computer.

Today we can use computers to make pictures. Colours, lines and shapes can be changed quickly and you can repeat patterns easily. If you have a good printer the results can be very exciting.

Mixing colours

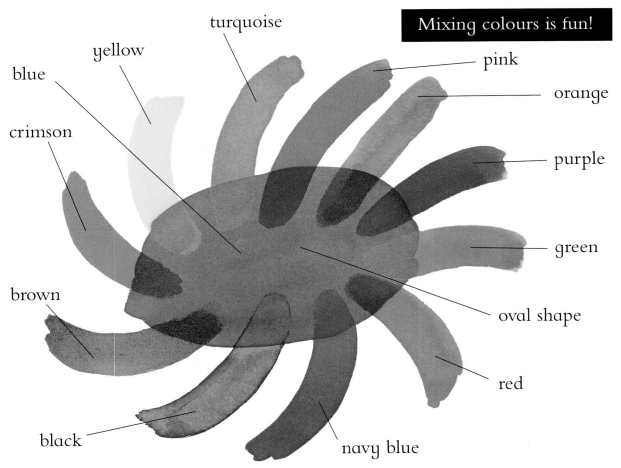

Mixing colours is fun!

turquoise

yellow

blue

crimson

brown

black

pink

orange

purple

green

oval shape

red

navy blue

Use some paint to experiment with colours:

1. Choose a primary colour and add other colours to it.
2. Keep a record of the colours you mix together and the new colours they make.
3. Use the different colours you have made to paint something simple like sky or water.

How many colours do you think there are? 10? 20? 100? 1000? More?

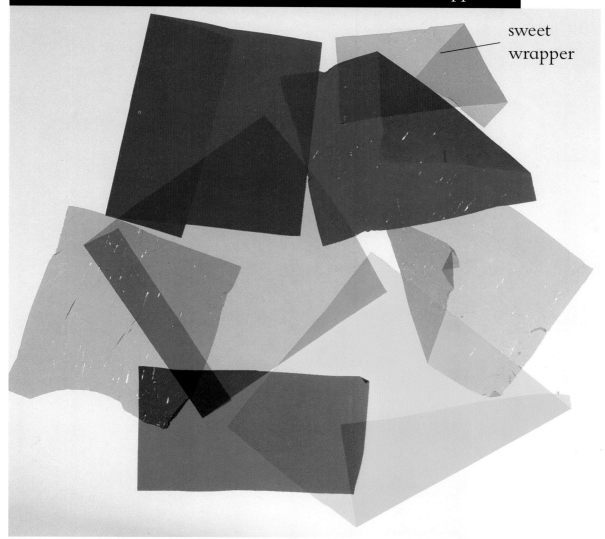

sweet wrapper

Now try this:

1. Collect see-through coloured sweet wrappers.
2. Tape some of the wrappers to a window and overlap them to make different colours.
3. Fold some wrappers in half to make stronger colours.

23

Colours working together

Decorated spinners.

When colours move, our eyes can see things which are not there. Spinning colours can have a strange effect. Make some simple spinners and decorate them. Use the **designs** shown here to help you.

24

You can make a spinner as follows:

1. Cut out a circle of card about 15 cm wide and ask an adult to make two holes about 1 cm from the centre.
2. Draw a design on one side and then colour it. Repeat the design on the other side but colour it differently.
3. Get some thin string or wool and thread it through the two holes. Knot the string to make a loop.

Hold the string in both hands, twist it and then gently pull. The card will spin and you will see the colours change.

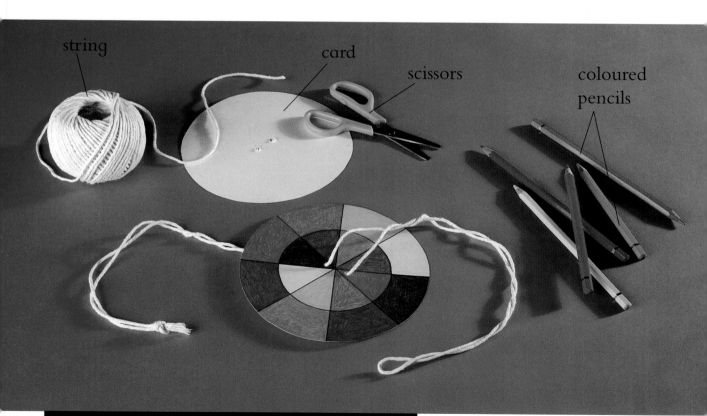

string   card   scissors   coloured pencils

You need these things to make a spinner.

Colours and tones

Adding white   Adding purple   Adding white   Adding green

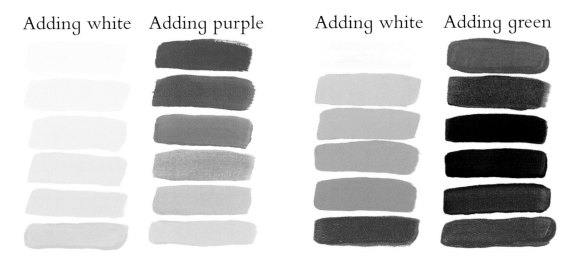

Adding white   Adding orange

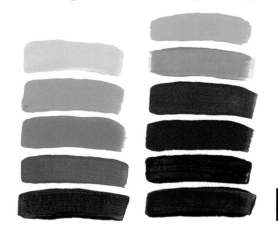

Tones that match each other on the ladders often work best together in paintings.

Different tone ladders.

Use paints to make tone ladders.
1. Put two big blobs of one of the primary colours onto a palette.
2. Add small amounts of white paint to one of the blobs.
3. Then add tiny amounts of the complementary colour to the other blob.
4. As you make different shades, add them to your tone ladder like the ones shown above.

Here Claude Monet has used the light and dark tones of purple, blue and green to paint his lily pond. Monet was interested in the way light and water **interacted** to keep changing the **scene**.

Monet painted his lily pond many times. Each picture is different.

blue

green

purple

waterlily

Claude Monet, *Waterlilies*, 1907.

27

Painting with dots

river bank

river

bather

Georges Pierre Seurat, *Bathers at Asnieres*, 1883-84.

Georges Seurat was an artist who **experimented** with colour in a **scientific** way. He used tiny dots of colour. Look at the boy on the right side of the picture. He seems surrounded with bright light. Seurat used light and dark **tones** and mixed them together to create this special effect.

Seurat's way of painting tricks us into seeing colours. The colours blend in our heads, not on the **canvas**! Try experimenting with tiny dots of coloured paint. Make a simple picture just using dots of colour – it is not as easy as it first looks!

29

Glossary

a b c d e f g h i j k l m n o p q r s t u v w x y z

Aborigine — native person of Australia

abstract — kind of art which does not try to show people or things, but instead uses shape and colour to make the picture

canvas — strong woven material on which many artists paint

combination — two or more things together

complement — make another colour seem bright

complementary colour — a colour opposite another on the colour wheel

contrasts — differences that you can see when things are compared

decorative — pleasant or interesting to look at

design — lines and shapes which decorate art

earth colour — warm colour found in nature, such as brown or red

experiment — try things out, or repeat something until you like the result

explore — examine how something works

hieroglyphs	pictures used by the ancient Egyptians instead of words
interact	how things work with each other
monastery	building where monks live and pray
overlap	partly cover
palette	board used to mix colours on
primary colour	red, blue and yellow – colours which cannot be made by mixing other colours
secondary colour	colour which is made by mixing two primary colours together
scene	view painted by an artist
scientific	like science, testing ideas in an ordered way
shade	a darker or lighter version of a colour
stained glass	small pieces of coloured glass put together to make a picture
tone	shades and depth of colour, from light to dark or dull to bright

a b c d e f g h i j k l m n o p q r s t u v w x y z

Index

EDUCATION LIBRARY SERVICE

Browning Way
Woodford Park Industrial Estate
Winsford
Cheshire CW7 2JN

Phone: 01606 592551/557126
Fax: 01606 861412
www.cheshire.gov.uk/els/home.htm

CHESHIRE
COUNTY COUNCIL
Education Library Service
Part of Community Development